JOY O
CHIP
CARVING

JOY OF
CHIP
CARVING

Step–by–Step Instructions & Designs from a **Master Carver**

WAYNE BARTON

Fox Chapel
PUBLISHING

To Marlies. The journey is miraculous.

© 2019 by Wayne Barton and Fox Chapel Publishing Company, Inc., 903 Square Street, Mount Joy, PA 17552.

Joy of Chip Carving is an original work, first published in 2019 by Fox Chapel Publishing Company, Inc. The patterns contained herein are copyrighted by the author. Readers may make copies of these patterns for personal use. The patterns themselves, however, are not to be duplicated for resale or distribution under any circumstances. Any such copying is a violation of copyright law.

ISBN 978-1-4971-0056-5

The Cataloging-in-Publication Data is on file with the Library of Congress.

To learn more about the other great books from Fox Chapel Publishing, or to find a retailer near you, call toll-free 800-457-9112 or visit us at *www.FoxChapelPublishing.com*.

We are always looking for talented authors. To submit an idea, please send a brief inquiry to acquisitions@foxchapelpublishing.com.

Printed in Singapore
First printing

Table of Contents

PAGE 11

PAGE 19

PAGE 22

Acknowledgments 7

Foreword 8

Introduction..9

Tools and Materials 11

Sharpening..12

How to Hold the Knives 13

    The Cutting Knife 13

    The Stab Knife 15

Carving Tips 16

Understanding Line and Design.............................19

    Definition of Lines 19

    Elements of Composition................................20

    Design Suggestions..21

Candleholder Project 22

Borders...31

The Barton Capitals...46

Foliated Alphabet..56

Gallery 67

About the Author...152

PAGE 46

PAGE 56

Acknowledgments

This book may be viewed as a journey through my chip carving career, which has been encouraged and inspired by an extraordinary number of talented people. I have enjoyed the warmth and pleasure of their friendship. Not wanting to risk the omission of any, I would like to say at once to all, thank you for what you have given and what we have shared. You know who you are.

Because this journey has been a long one, I must reach back in time to recognize a few in particular who traveled along with me influencing the work within these pages.

Though recently deceased, any acknowledgment would be incomplete without a mention of Gottlieb Siegfried Brandli, the master Swiss cabinetmaker and dear friend with whom I worked and traveled for more than thirty-five years. He designed and made the pieces I carved during this time.

"It is my intent and desire that all who use this sourcebook experience sparks of inspiration and encouragement."

An acknowledgment of my very long, hearty friendship and collaboration with Roger Strautman specifically needs mention. We have worked together and collaborated on numerous carving projects. His bright and cheerful sense of humor always made each one a delightful experience and always has me looking forward to the next.

Equally important, my long association with Rick Switzer has treated me to bountiful, fresh conversations that are both enriching and intuitive, reaching far beyond design and carving. We have traveled extensively teaching classes together. Besides being a superb carver, his genial, insightful nature makes him the perfect instructor.

David Crothers, Bruce Nicholas, Joey Wade, and Bill Johnson, all creative artists and carvers, have been dedicated to this journey and have kept me company along the way. So, too, I'd like to thank my daughter Heidi, who properly challenged without reservation my peculiar English phrasing while taking on the task of proofreading/correcting, and typing dictation faster than I can talk.

For many years "the woman behind the curtain" who has been a trusted consultant successfully steering my business activities is my dear friend and webmaster, Kim Penny. Hers is the rare combination of being patient, intuitive, and clever (her spot-on company name is CyberSizzle Media), with a sweetness that puts a smile on the road ahead.

A very grateful expression of appreciation must be given to my editors, Bud Sperry and Jeremy Hauck. Their professional advice, suggestions, and patience skillfully ensured this project to proceed with illumination and understanding.

Lastly, above all else, I have a poverty of words to express the deepest love and gratitude to my wife Marlies for her endearing support to this project, which she has done so many times in the past. From the very beginning of my journey her physical, emotional and intellectual assistance and presence has always guided my footsteps.

Foreword

This book represents the sharing of one man's ongoing insights and lifetime study of the unique art of chip carving.

Wayne Barton is the most renowned proponent of this style of woodcarving in the world. He has been honored by the Swiss National Museum in Zurich, which put his work on special exhibition for eighteen months. In 2005 Fox Chapel Publishing named him Woodcarver of the Year. His classes, lectures, and writings for decades have taught countless others like you the proper tools and methods used to accomplish superb chip carvings such as those displayed within these pages. With few exceptions, most individuals in North America who are passing on chip carving knowledge were introduced to the art by Wayne and/or his classes and writings. However, it remains true today that none have reached Wayne's level in either range or depth of execution, techniques, and artistic design, nor equaled his remarkable ability to describe and instruct others in chip carving.

Singlehandedly, Wayne Barton has been the driving force behind the recognition and renaissance that chip carving has enjoyed both here and abroad. Owing to his inspired example, chip carving is today commonplace in nearly all woodcarving shows, to the point of comprising a distinct category in most competitions.

Introduced to woodcarving at the age of five by his Norwegian grandfather, Wayne has had a love for the art and for the process of carving ever since. With a serious desire to increase his knowledge, he went to Brienz, Switzerland studying all forms of woodcarving under the tutelage of some of the masters still actively carving and teaching there. Upon his return to the United States, he taught at the Chicago School of Woodcarving before establishing the Alpine School of Woodcarving,

Ltd. with chip carving as a specialty. Although he was awarded first place in every competition he entered, his focus has always been on teaching and sharing his knowledge with others. Additionally, he has spotlighted the talents and accomplishments of chip carving students from around the globe for the past thirty-five years in his bimonthly column in Chip Chats, the National Woodcarvers Magazine.

Long before anyone else, Wayne recognized the need for superior chip carving tools. As a result, he developed the Wayne Barton Premier Chip Carving Knives, which are now in common use worldwide and recognized as the best available for their superior quality and ergonomic design. He has also developed popular easy-to-use ceramic sharpening stones that are unsurpassed in quality.

With no more than two knives and his extraordinary skills, Wayne Barton has introduced us to the unique art form of chip carving. He continues to create his magnificent carvings, which are enjoyed and copied by so many others.

I am fortunate to be one of the many carvers who engaged in the practice of chip carving. This was made possible entirely through the writings of Wayne Barton on this carving specialty. The pages that follow present the eighth book Wayne has written on the subject. It is the culmination of more than fifty years of his chip carving knowledge and artistic insights. Having been exposed to the entire spectrum of chip carving information available over the past twenty-some years, I can attest to the fact that the following pages cannot be equaled for advancing your knowledge and skills. Read, observe, practice and enjoy.

David W. Crothers
Souderton, Pennsylvania

Introduction

𝕿he essence of chip carving is simplicity and versatility. It is a decorative style of carving quickly and it is easily learned. It is simple in tool use and execution, and versatile in design possibilities and application. Its name is derived from the carving process. Chip carving does not create objects but rather applies various decoration and embellishment to that which already exists, such as a box, plate, furniture, etc. In chip carving, precise cuts are incised into the wood, forming chips of various geometric shapes, sizes, and proportions. Design aside, good chip carving is distinguished by its execution of single-angle smooth facets, clean grooves, and sharp ridges.

PREFERRED TOOLS AND WOOD

All the carvings within these pages were executed with only two knives, the Premier Chip Carving Knives I designed many years ago (see page 11). Today their truly superior quality is recognized worldwide for their blades of high carbon tool steel, and handles ergonomically designed for hours of comfortable, enjoyable carving.

The woods employed in this book are primarily basswood (genus *Tilia*) of the linden family, often considered by some since the Middle Ages as the queen of carving woods; and butternut (*Juglans cinera*) of the walnut family, also known as white walnut. These woods, both classified as hardwoods, are commonly selected for chip carving. Not for their softer nature alone but also for their straight, tight grain.

JOY OF CHIP CARVING

POSITIVE IMAGE

As a young man, an extraordinary opportunity to formally study woodcarving in Brienz, Switzerland, the Swiss woodcarving center, presented itself to me. Such good fortune put me in close proximity to Europe's castles and cathedrals, allowing also an additional study of medieval art and architecture. Without disregarding the traditional geometric aspects of chip carving, it was this study that inspired me to develop what has been called "positive image." This is the practice of using chip carving techniques to remove wood around an image to give it a positive attitude (as one might do in relief carving), as opposed to more traditional incising of an image into the wood producing a negative expression. The positive image concept presented in numerous examples herein, such as the **foliated alphabet (see page 56)**, extends the parameters of chip carving to dimensions that are evolutionary, expansive, and exciting. However, the distinction between positive and negative may not always be obvious and elaborate explanation risks confusion, particularly if the two are designed together, rendering debate on the subject moot (the right design in the picture below).

While this book has specific instructional sections considered pertinent to all visual arts including chip carving, it was conceived more as a broad sampling and overview of a lifetime of study, understanding, and practice of the unlimited design possibilities in artful chip carving in both geometric and positive image. Rather than long explanations and duplicating drawings, it provides a photo gallery of diverse avenues a viewer may study for specific purposes or just to peruse for inspirational pleasure.

It is my intent and desire that all who use this sourcebook experience sparks of inspiration and encouragement.

Left: traditional incising of an image into wood. Right: positive image produced by removing wood around an image.

Tools and Materials

While the knives used for chip carving through the ages have varied to accommodate different methods and styles, their number has always been few. In some cases, chisels and gouges were, and still are, used. Today, my toolkit couldn't be simpler. As previously mentioned, only the two Wayne Barton Premier Chip Carving Knives were used to carve all the work that is shown in this book. No other knives are needed. I also have in my kit two ceramic sharpening stones to keep my blades sharp and polished. Additionally, a .05 mechanical pencil with grade B lead, an eraser, small T-square, and a bow compass, also with grade B lead, will round out my toolkit.

In addition to these tools, transferring designs to the wood will require transfer paper, graphite paper, and a stylus.

TOOL TIP

The Premier Chip Carving Knives and ceramic sharpening stones recommended are available from:

Alpine School of Woodcarving
225 Vine Ave.
Park Ridge, IL 60068
847-692-2822
www.chipcarving.com

Clockwise from top: eraser, .05 mechanical pencil, T-square, ceramic sharpening stones, Wayne Barton Premier Chip Carving Knives (stab knife bottom, cutting knife top), bow compass.

Sharpening

A poorly sharpened knife can deprive you of the *joy of chip carving*. There are three criteria to the process of sharpening: producing a sharp cutting edge, sharpening at the correct angle, and producing a blade that is highly polished without a burr on the edge or a hook on the tip.

Chip carving, unlike all other forms of carving that are executed by shaving wood, calls for the carver to insert the blade into the wood to remove specific shapes, pieces, or chips. The angle at which the blade is sharpened is critical.

Flat ceramic sharpening stones (not rods) are best. They are so hard that even with extended use they remain flat. Unlike natural stones, the high quality of the ceramic stone is uniform and constant. Further, the ceramic stone requires no oil or water as lubricant in the sharpening process.

Sharpen the cutting knife first on the medium-grade stone, keeping equal pressure on the heel and tip of the blade. Raise the blade about the thickness of a credit card under the back edge of the blade and with a back-and-forth sliding movement sharpen on one side of the stone and then equally on the other. Bring the edge to a slight burr. Continue as before but with less pressure until the burr disappears. Check light reflection by holding the knife under a bright light with your finger on the tip, to cut any glare. When there is no burr and you see no light reflecting off the edge, the knife is ready for polishing.

Use the ultra-fine ceramic stone to hone each side equally so that you don't create a burr. Polishing the metal in this way will assure that the blade will glide easily through the wood rather than drag.

Check for light reflection again, and cut diagonally across the grain of a piece of scrap wood to check for drag. Your knife should flow smoothly and steadily.

The stab knife is sharpened with the same stones and procedures used for the cutting knife, with the exception of the sharpening angle. The angle for the stab knife is approximately thirty degrees and is established at the factory. Because the stab knife is used only for impressing or indenting the wood to enhance a design, the angle of the cutting edge is more crucial than its sharpness.

The frequency of sharpening will depend on the quality of the steel in your blades, the variety of wood being used, and the type of cuts being made. Some kinds of wood can dull a blade quickly, and deep and curved cuts can wear an edge more quickly.

You will develop a feel for when it is time to hone your blades on the ultra-fine stone. You will find yourself using more pressure to get the same results than you did initially. Also, you will notice that light begins to reflect from the edge as it dulls. To freshen the edges, normally using only the ultra-fine stone will suffice to sharpen the cutting edge.

How to Hold the Knives

All hand tools are made to be used and held in a particular fashion. The Premier Chip Carving Knives are no exception. Though it may feel strange or even awkward at first, with a little practice it will soon become apparent that holding the knives in a correct manner will make carving infinitely easier, faster, safer, and a far more pleasant experience.

Whether carving in the first or second position, some part of the carving hand should always be in contact with the wood. In the first position it will be the thumb bracing, pivoting or sliding on the flat part of the handle while carving. In the second position, dropping the first finger to the wood will suffice.

THE CUTTING KNIFE

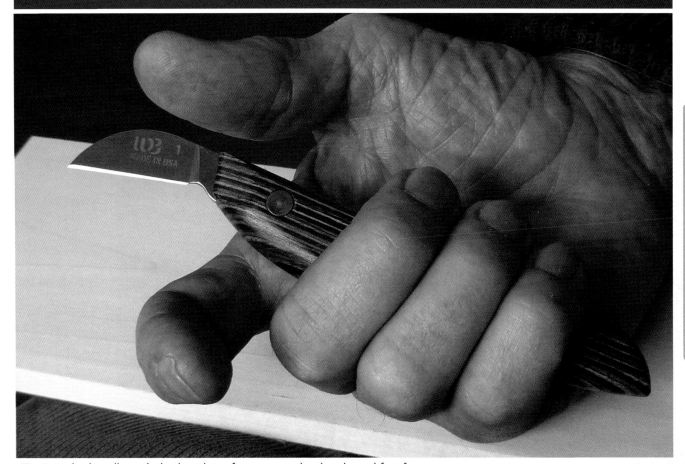

1 Grip the handle with the last three fingers, not the thumb and first finger. Gripping the knife properly this way will give you more control and power when carving. Next, close the hand around the handle. Then roll the wrist outward while keeping the elbow next to the body for better leverage and to ensure the knife is drawn toward the body and not across it.

2 There is a flattened area on either side of the handle (for both right- and left-handed carvers) located on the underside next to the blade. Place the knuckle of the thumb at the end of the flattened area by the blade with the thumb turned outward from the handle. Positioning the thumb here will provide a fulcrum for the knife while carving. The length of the flattened area allows the thumb to slide easily when it is necessary to raise the blade when carving. Held properly, the blade should normally be at a 65-degree angle for most carving.

When carving in the first or predominant position, always keep the thumb against the handle, as opposed to carving, as one does when peeling potatoes, by drawing the blade toward the thumb. By keeping the thumb against the handle, the correct angle is locked in place and the blade can never cut the thumb by being pulled into it. Also, when the thumb is held against the handle, the knife can only be moved by pulling from the shoulder, giving you much greater strength and control while carving.

HOW NOT TO HOLD A KNIFE

This illustrates incorrect positioning of the thumb. The knife should not be pulled to the thumb as one does when peeling potatoes. Always keep your thumb against the handle.

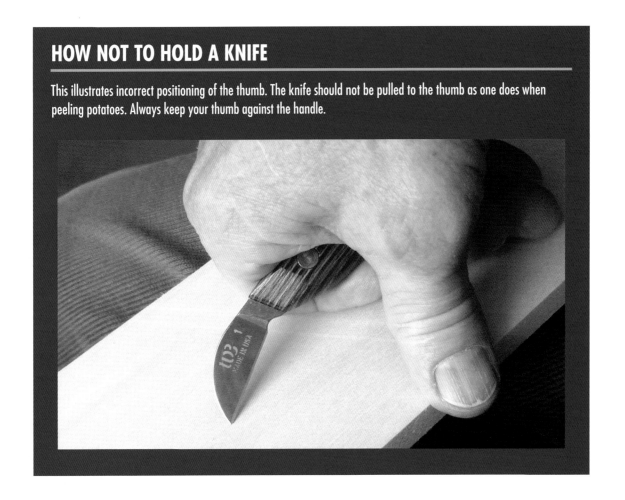

3 The second position is used primarily when making smaller three corner or triangular chips, and notches made with two cuts. The second position is accomplished by placing the first thumb knuckle on the spine of the blade at the blade end of the handle. Closing the hand around the handle and placing the hand down on the wood will put the blade approximately at a 65-degree angle opposite that of the first position.

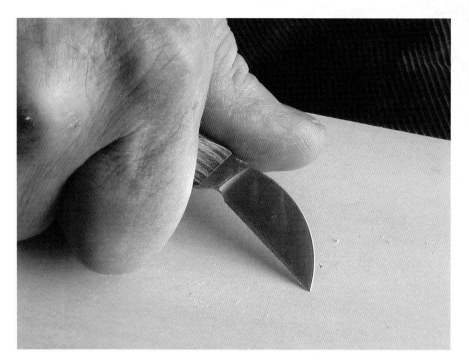

THE STAB KNIFE

The stab knife is held by one or two hands perpendicular to the wood with the blade edge toward the carver. It is thrust downward to make an impression deep enough to cut the wood fibers, and rocked on its edge to extend the impression to whatever length desired. This normally is made in a single movement. When using the stab knife, the elbow should be kept close to the body. This will give you added leverage and strength from the shoulder.

Carving Tips

1. Traditionally, chip carving was done in a sitting position, and working on the lap. It is still the best way to do this style of carving. To work on a table or bench is to forfeit leverage and strength, and is not recommended. The only exception to this rule would be if the piece being carved is too large to hold on the lap. Choose a comfortable chair that allows both feet to rest on the ground and also makes your lap level to the ground.

2. If artificial lighting is being used, a shaded articulating desk lamp adjusted below eye level works well. Any light from above eye level may cause glare, making carving details sometimes difficult to see, and is tiring for the eyes.

3. In preparing wood for carving, sand the surface with the grain with no finer than **220-grit paper**. This allows designs to be more easily drawn directly on the wood. It is also easier to clean off any pencil lines left after carving. Carving off pencil lines in the carving process of removing chips also simplifies cleanup. When removing pencil or graphite marks use an eraser. Trying to sand them off may drive the graphite into the wood grain.

4. Before attempting any projects, working on practice boards is a good idea. Practicing the rudiments and basic motifs of chip carving will make any project much less formidable and intimidating. Avoid over designing or carving a composition. Leave some un-carved visual breathing space. Simplicity often makes the best statement.

5. Because the blade is held at a constant angle, the wider the chip, the deeper the cut must be made to relieve it. Conversely, a small or narrow chip needs only the tip of the blade to remove it. Cutting deeper than necessary to remove a chip may relieve wood not intended to be removed.

If a chip does not release freely, cut it loose, do not pry.

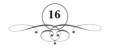

6. There are occasions when a chip may be too large to remove in a single pass. In this case, cut as normal, removing the top portion of the chip. When removing the remaining part of the chip, be sure the blade is held at the same angle as the original angle for all subsequent cuts.

7. For consistently clean and good-looking results in carving, with a few exceptions, hold the blade at an angle of approximately **65 degrees**. Cutting too shallow an angle makes the carving appear flat and lifeless because a lack of shadows will hide the carving. Cutting too steep an angle will make it difficult, if not impossible, to remove chips, and render any ridges in the design weak.

8. When making straight-line cuts, let the hand ride on the thumb and knuckle of the first finger as it guides the knife through the wood. Straight lines can be made quite easily if focus is concentrated about a half-inch (13 mm) in front of the blade instead of on the blade itself, letting the eye "pull" the blade.

9. The use of a straightedge to assist in cutting a straight line is not recommended. A tool in each hand dramatically increases the possibility of an error, particularly if the straightedge inadvertently moves.

10. When making curved cuts, raise the blade to a more vertical position while maintaining the 65-degree cutting angle. This maneuver will reduce the amount of blade edge in the wood, allowing clean, smooth cuts to be made in curves. The tighter the curve, the higher the blade will need to be raised.

11. The Premier cutting knife, with its thin tapering blade tempered for toughness, will carve very well for many years with proper care. However, if a chip does not release from the wood cleanly, it is because all the fibers have not been severed. While it may be tempting to pry the chip out, the blade is not designed to function in this manner, and prying with it runs the risk of breaking off the tip. If a chip does not release freely, cut it loose, do not pry.

12. With few exceptions, when carving, make the first cut of a new chip away from ones already carved. This will help prevent wood not intended to be removed from splitting. If any wood breaks out and needs to be glued back, a dab of **white glue** will do nicely. Be careful not to get any on the surface, as it will leave a clear spot if stain is later used.

13. When non-geometric designs or patterns such as those representing foliage are to be transferred, they are best drawn on **tracing paper** first. Being able to see through the paper allows the pattern to be positioned perfectly on the wood. Place **graphite paper** between the wood and the tracing paper, and with a **stylus** trace the pattern onto the wood. The use of carbon paper should be avoided because the colored wax transmitted from this material can permanently stain the wood.

14. It is not recommended to glue a pattern onto the wood and carve through the paper. While this may appear to be a shortcut as one prepares to carve, it has serious drawbacks. It is impossible to see through the paper to position it properly on the wood or during the process of carving. While carving, wood that was not intended to be removed may split or be cut. Even if transparent paper is used, the same result may occur and not be discovered until the paper is removed. Having the paper move or come loose during carving is also a concern. Removing adhesive after the paper is lifted is not only bothersome, but also raises the possibility of damaging the carving.

With few exceptions, when carving, make the first cut of a new chip away from ones already carved.

Understanding Line and Design

The ability to understand and create design is within all of us. Writing is an example of how design is understood and copied. Our interpretation of letters is the creative aspect of the process.

The analysis of lines that define or represent objects usually takes place at the subconscious level.

What exactly is design? In the consideration of chip carving (as well as many other disciplines), design may be described as resolving or defining geometric shapes, patterns, and motifs, usually in a pleasing manner based on certain principles and concepts. Just as music has auditory rhythm, there is a visual rhythm and flow to good design. This is accomplished by line alone. A dash and a dot are recognized as segments of a line. The elements of composition, which incorporate basic geometric shapes such as triangles, circles, and squares, also include the concepts of contrast, balance, proportion, focal point, and movement.

Because we recognize objects by their "outline," the quality (length, direction) and quantity (number) of all lines is significant. A single dot will alter the impact of design. The analysis of lines that define or represent objects usually takes place at the subconscious level. To understand how and why lines affect our preferences and interpretations, we need to bring the elements of design composition to the conscious level.

When considering design for our purpose, a line may be described as having four attitudes: horizontal, vertical, diagonal, and curved. Each conveys a particular expression to which we respond because of our interpretation of past experiences or learned symbols. Combined, they form the geometric shapes and suggestions that are the foundation of decorative design.

DEFINITION OF LINES

- ❖ **Horizontal lines** represent rest and tranquility, a strong base, stability and steadiness.

- ❖ **Vertical lines** also represent stability. They are the opposite of the horizontal line, and complement it perfectly by forming with it squares and rectangles—the two basic geometric shapes of nearly all architectural structure. Vertical lines additionally represent awareness and alertness and have an uplifting quality, as observed in Gothic architecture.

- ❖ **Diagonal lines** are in transitional movement between vertical and horizontal stability, thereby expressing the exertion of energy. The visual energy and movement expressed by a diagonal line may be subtle or severe depending on its angle.

- ❖ **Curved lines** represent constant movement of various degrees determined by the radius, expressed perfectly by a circle.

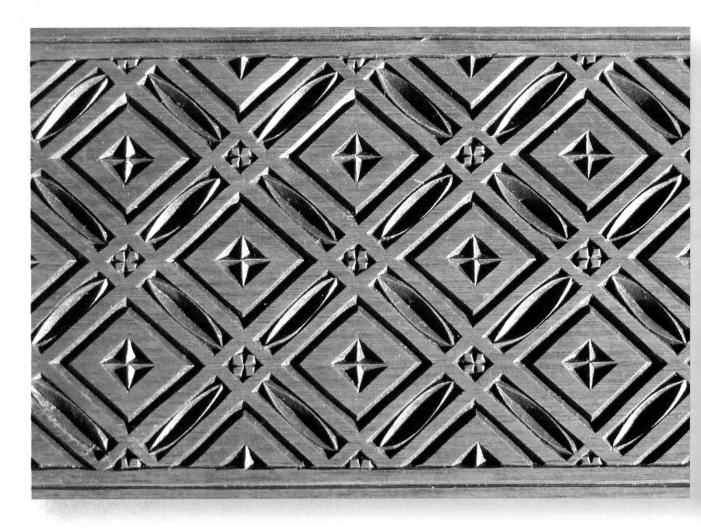

ELEMENTS OF COMPOSITION

Contrast, balance, proportion, focal point, and movement assist in arranging lines and shapes so that they are visually pleasing. Knowing and recognizing these elements is essential to good design.

Contrast helps define one item from another. The uncarved area of a chip-carved piece defines that which is carved. This is contrast. At times it is appropriate to have all lines or chips the same in a motif to produce a particular effect or feeling as found in many borders. But if this is contrasted within the overall design—large and small, straight and curved, square and round, etc.—the composition is extended to another level. Contrast within a composition will cause a carving to be more compelling.

Balance is counterpoise, equilibrium, an arrangement wherein opposing forces neutralize each other. Visual balance can, but need not, be symmetrical. A seven-point rosette is considered asymmetrical but is easily placed in a balanced position. Baroque architecture exemplifies the complete rejection of symmetry but is in perfect visual balance. No matter what other elements are brought into a design, visual balance will create steadiness.

Proportion is related to balance through equipoise, a visual weighting in size, number, and distance of the various parts of a design. When symmetrical, proportion demands that the parts be equal in all ways. When asymmetrical, the parts need be of a proportion to each other to maintain visual balance.

Focal point refers to that place or area to where the eye is first drawn naturally and continues to return as it takes in the entire design. Nearly always this will be the center of a piece. It may be a dot, a letter, a circle, or a complete rosette. It dominates the composition simply or elaborately and all else complements and supports it.

Movement, created by diagonal and curved lines, adds excitement and energy to a composition. Diagonal lines may form triangles or diamonds while curves may form circles or ovals.

DESIGN SUGGESTIONS

❖ Being consciously aware of the elements of design, their effects and interpretations, will greatly assist in their incorporation. Awareness is the key.

❖ Create chips that are carveable. Don't make them too large for the thickness of the wood to be carved.

❖ Leave visual breathing space. Usually it is not a good idea to carve every millimeter of wood in a design. The uncarved area will give definition to that which is carved within a composition.

❖ Placing a border too close to the edge of a piece often will cause the carving to appear cramped and ill-conceived.

❖ Create chips that relate to, and complement, each other. They should not appear as though they are floating aimlessly.

❖ To achieve a visual third dimension effect, avoid assigning the same value to all the lines (chips) to be carved. Vary the width of your lines.

❖ A design is best when not "read" in a moment's glance. Employing the various elements and concepts of design will create interest. The visual communication between artist and audience is, and should be, a joyful, enduring encounter.

AN EASY STEP-BY-STEP EXPLANATION:

Candleholder Project

To illustrate the step-by-step process of layout, carving, and finishing, a 10" (254 mm) basswood candle plate with an outside bead and a 3" (76 mm) center hole to accommodate a candle is chosen. The numbered steps showing the order of drawing and removing chips is fairly common to most projects of this nature, with exceptions acknowledged. It is important that time is given to layout for accuracy. Clarity of design is the hallmark of fine chip carving. When drawing, use the softer grade "B" lead in both pencil and compass and avoid making dark heavy lines. This will make any necessary erasing much easier.

See page 30 for the patterns used to make this project.

The finishing process illustrated and explained herein is certainly not the only method but it is tried and true and must be given the same care and consideration as the layout and carving. All the pieces shown within these pages that are stained were finished as described below. For best results, it is strongly suggested to first finish a carved practice board of the same kind of wood as the carving to be finished before attempting work on an actual piece.

All staining herein is done with oil-based gel stain (my preference is General Finishes Oil Based Gel Stain for its quality and broad choice of colors. Minwax gel stains are not recommended.). General Gel Stain is chosen for its workability and compatibility with other finishing products used. Also, all pieces herein are sprayed on (not brushed) and if an HVLP (high volume low pressure) spray unit is not available, I like Minwax Satin Fast Drying Polyurethane in a spray can. Always spray in a well-vented area wearing protection equipment.

LAYOUT

1 Locate the center of the plate. All major circles within the design will use this point (note: a center finder was used here and the author is left-handed).

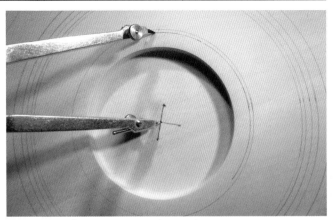

2 Draw all necessary circles to the correct predetermined sizes and positions.

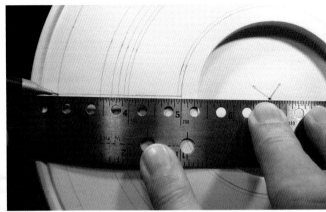

3 Orient a ruler horizontally with the wood grain and draw a line on both sides of the center point.

4 To bisect the line drawn in no. 3, place the compass point as shown on both sides of the center to create the Xs. Place a ruler connecting the center of the Xs and draw lines on both sides of the plate center as done previously.

STEP-BY-STEP

JOY OF CHIP CARVING

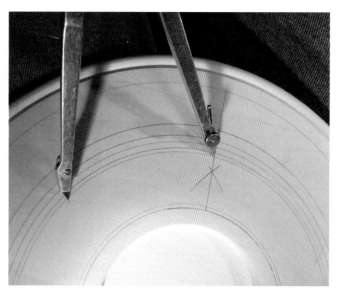

5 Setting the original radius of the circle shown, place the compass point at that intersection and mark the radius on the circle. Without removing the compass point, swing the compass over to the other side and mark the circle again. Now place the compass point on the opposite side where the straight line again meets the circle and repeat marking the circle as before. This will produce six equal sections marked on the circle.

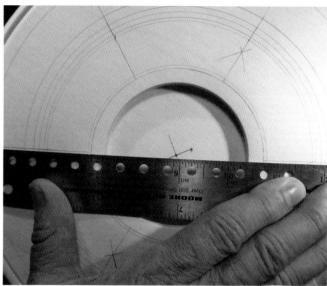

6 Place a ruler across the center connecting the remaining points marked on the circle and draw a line on both sides of the center as previously. This will create twelve equally spaced lines on the circle.

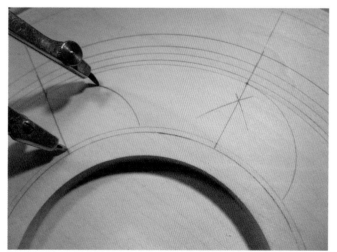

7 Reset your compass radius and draw a quarter circle at every other line.

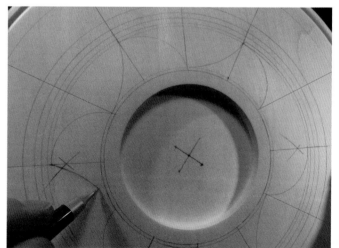

8 In the remaining spaces between the quarter circles, hand draw a slow curve from the top of one to the bottom of the next.

9 By hand divide each section into four equal segments.
Hint: *first divide a segment in half and then in half again.*

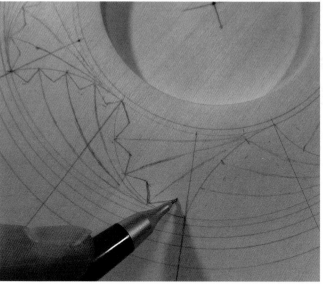

10 Draw a pyramid on the end of each segment.

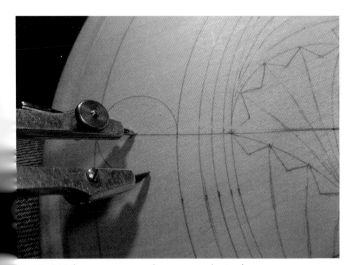

11 With a compass draw a circle in the outer area on every other line.

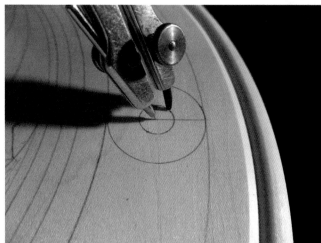

12 Add a smaller circle inside the larger one.

JOY OF CHIP CARVING

13 Trace the foliated design onto tracing paper (you may have to adjust the design for your use). Using the circles to center your tracing, secure the tracing paper to the plate. Slip a piece of graphite paper under the tracing paper and with a stylus transfer the pattern to the plate. Repeat around the plate producing six transfers of the foliated design. Draw the flowers within the circles.

14 Lastly, in the row designated for a boarder of three cornered chips, divide each section to receive eight chips using the simple dot method.

CARVING

In the carving phase, the larger chips of the motif which may be called a negative image are removed first. This is not because of their position within the design but because they are the largest. Generally, removing larger chips first helps to eliminate wood splitting or cracking as work progresses.

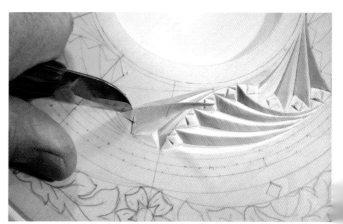

15 The first chips removed are those creating the negative motif around the center hole. The first cuts made on these elongated chips are the two made on the wide end of each chip. The second cut is made from the wide end of the chip to the narrow end. It is easier to insert the blade to the necessary depth and draw it out as the chip narrows. Be aware of cutting deeper that necessary to relieve a chip. Excessive undercutting relieves wood meant to be saved.

16 The third, or relieving, cut that frees the chip is a shallow cut from the narrow end of the chip to the wide end, inserting the blade as the chip gets wider. Whenever possible, make the first cut on a new chip away from a previously removed chip. Note that the narrow ends of each group of four do not all go to a single point but rather are staggered. This helps to keep each chip intact.

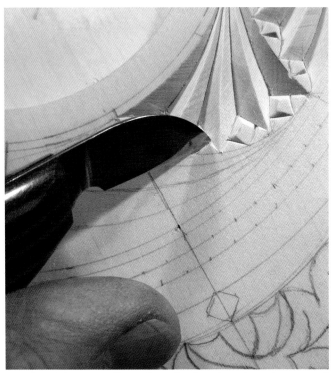

17 Make a small notch on both sides of each pyramid as shown.

18 Cut the small rings on either side of the negative motif. Note how shallow the tip of the blade is inserted.

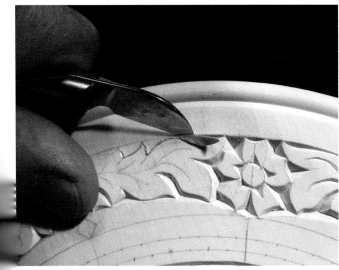

19 Relieve the foliated motif by cutting around it first, then make the relieving cut on both borders of the motif last. Cutting in this order will his will keep the edges smoother.

20 Remove the elongated chip to reveal the diamond under the foliated motif.

STEP-BY-STEP · JOY OF CHIP CARVING

21 Use the stab knife to accent the petals of the flowers.

22 Relieve the ring of three-cornered chips.

FINISHING

The two woods used for carving in this book are basswood and butternut. Because these are both softer hardwoods, special care must be given to preparation before staining. At about a 45-degree angle, spray an even coat of the recommended polyurethane on the carving as a sealer coat. Note: If you have end grain to stain, this area will need more spray. Continue to give end grain more "shots" until the wood stops absorbing the spray. Next, immediately take a shop rag and wipe the entire carving. This will remove any excess spray and leave an even coat. When dry, very lightly sand any areas of raised grain with 220 grit and dust off thoroughly.

23. Using a fairly stiff artist's brush with about one-inch bristles, rapidly apply the gel stain liberally.

24 Once on, do not let it sit. With a shop cloth, wipe all excess gel off immediately.

25 Continue to wipe out and wipe off all excess gel. If you observe any bare spots missed, use only gel remaining on the carving. Do not go back into the can for more gel, it has more solvent and will remove the still-wet gel on the carving. Wait until the gel on the carving is dry, then it is safe to go back into the can for a dab of gel to cover any bare spots. If a deeper color is desired, repeat the staining process for a second coat.

26 When all is dry, check for any raised grain then spray a final thin coat or two of the satin polyurethane for a soft, rich appearance.

Ring dimensions for 10" plate

Beaded edge

3" recessed circle for candle

1/16"

1/16"

1/8"

7/8"

1/4"

1"

1/8"

3/16"

5/16"

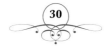

Foliated motif for candle plate.

Borders

In chip carving (as well as other disciplines), the general essence and function of a border is to frame and visually contain that which is within its boundary. It is an artistic device to prevent the eye from wandering beyond its parameters, keeping a focused eye harnessed. While not always necessary, a border often will give better or clearer vision and comprehension to an entire composition.

A border may be as simple as a single line or something far more elaborate. It may be positive or negative or a combination of both. The examples shown here are carved on frames, boxes, and plates selected to illustrate broad design diversity and possibilities.

1 Make a copy of the design on tracing paper so that you may be able to see how to place the design correctly on the wood piece to be carved. Place graphite paper between the tracing paper and the wood. Use a stylus to transfer the design to the wood. When finished, remove both the tracing paper and graphite papers.

2 Carve the border and when completed, erase any remaining pencil and graphite marks. Do not try to sand off these marks as you may drive the graphite into the wood grain.

3 9" × 12" (23 × 30 cm) frame, board width is 3" (76 mm). Note the corner treatments and how easily the vine length is visually changed by adding or subtracting a leaf section in the vine. (basswood)

BORDER DESIGNS

12" (30 cm) anniversary plate with curved vine motif. (basswood)

12" (30 cm) plate with Celtic knot border complementing center compass rose. (basswood)

18" (45 cm) lazy Susan, combined flower and leaf border. (butternut)

21¼" × 15½" (54 × 39 cm), board width is 3" (7 cm). Oil painting of family farm in Switzerland named *Sonnhalde* ("sunny side of the hill"). (basswood)

16" (40 cm) plate, alternating positive leaf and negative fan border. (basswood)

12" (30 cm) plate, positive leaf and ribbon borders. (basswood)

Geometric design on overlapping frame, 19¼" × 23" (49 × 58 cm), board width is 2" (5 cm). Pictured is master cabinet maker Gottlieb Siegfried Brandli. (basswood)

Bottom board piece
of frame, ribbon,
and diamond motif.
(basswood)

Corner motif of
frame. (basswood)

Frame 18" × 14" (45 × 35 cm), an example of multiple motifs within a single frame. (basswood)

If the stones are removed, The brook will lose its song.

12" (30 cm) plate, combined flower and leaf design. (basswood)

Box lid, 13" × 8½" (33 × 21 cm), combined negative line and leaf border. (basswood)

14" (35 cm) square frame, board width is 3½" (9 cm). Center is a terrazzo tile from my wife's childhood home in Hinwil, Switzerland. (basswood)

Frame 9" × 7" (23 × 18 cm), board width is 1½" (4 cm). Note the foliated lettering of "friends" within the vine. From left: Marlies and Wayne Barton, Pamela and Arthur Aveling. (basswood)

8" (20 cm) plate, "flip-flop" negative fan border. (basswood)

Frame with vine motif 21" × 17" (53 × 43 cm), board width is 3" (7 cm). Note corner treatments. This picture is not a photo, but rather a colored pencil drawing with all fine features and details by Wayne Barton, of his companion of 16 years. (basswood)

12" (30 cm) double-beaded rim plate with crosshatch border and floral center in the Italian renaissance style. (basswood)

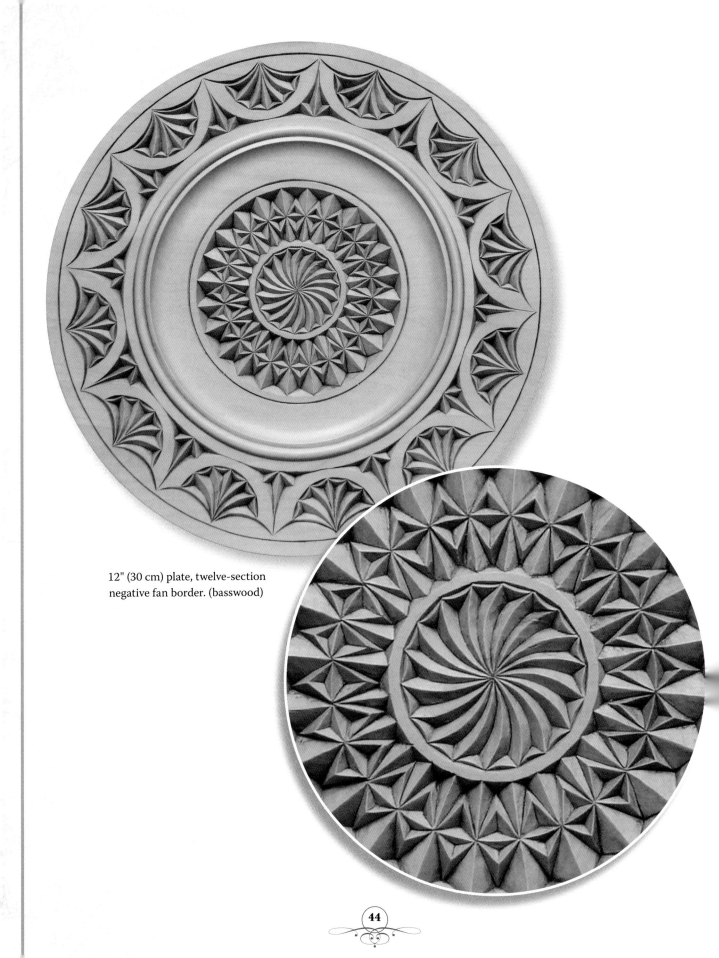

12" (30 cm) plate, twelve-section negative fan border. (basswood)

12" (30 cm) plate, pierced and sculpted, altering flower and crosshatched border. (butternut)

The Barton Capitals

This font was designed by me (Wayne Barton) without a lower case. Its primary purpose in development was to provide a legible yet ornamental style of capital letters. The letters are bold enough to stand alone when used as a single initial or together with others within a monogram. These capitals are designed for easy carving while maintaining an interesting style, particularly when used in a larger format. Furthermore, because of their bold ornamental style, they may also be used as a tasteful and artistically correct replacement or substitute of the capital letters in some other fonts that have both upper and lowercase letters.

A B C D E

F G H I J

K L M N N

O P Q R

S T U V

W X Y Z

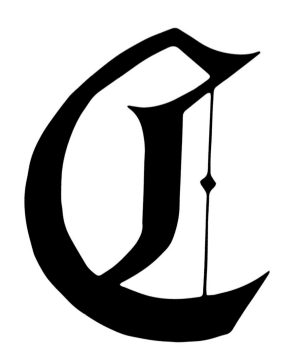

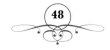

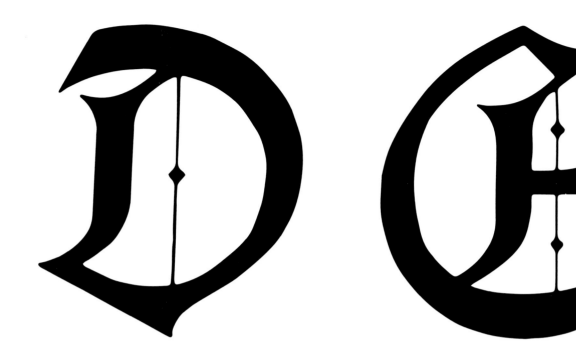

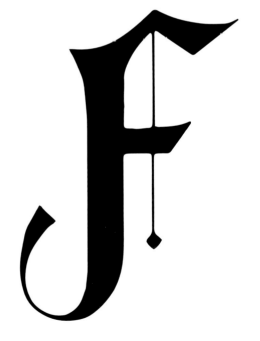

A I

J K

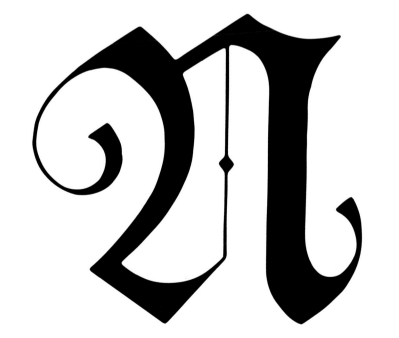

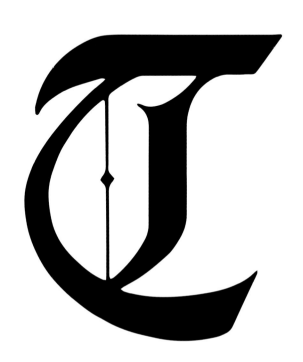

JOY OF CHIP CARVING

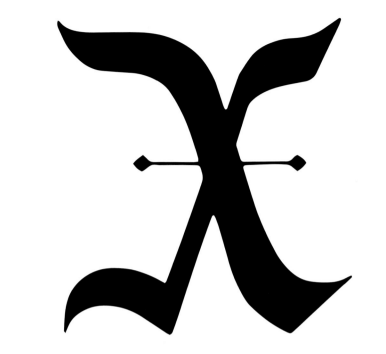

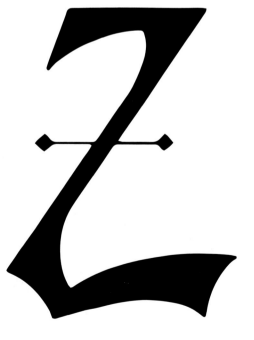

JOY OF CHIP CARVING

Foliated Alphabet

This foliated alphabet was designed and drawn by me (Wayne Barton). The foliated letter plaque was carved by Roger Strautman. The variations from one letter to another certainly indicate this is only one of many foliated alphabet possibilities. Each letter was originally created within a 3½" (13 mm) diameter circle and carved within a 2¾" (7 cm) diameter circle, all done in a positive image style. Note: while the letters are large, the chips to reveal the letters and leaves are relatively small. When designing, always remember to design chips that you can carve cleanly, comfortably, and which fit the context of the overall composition.

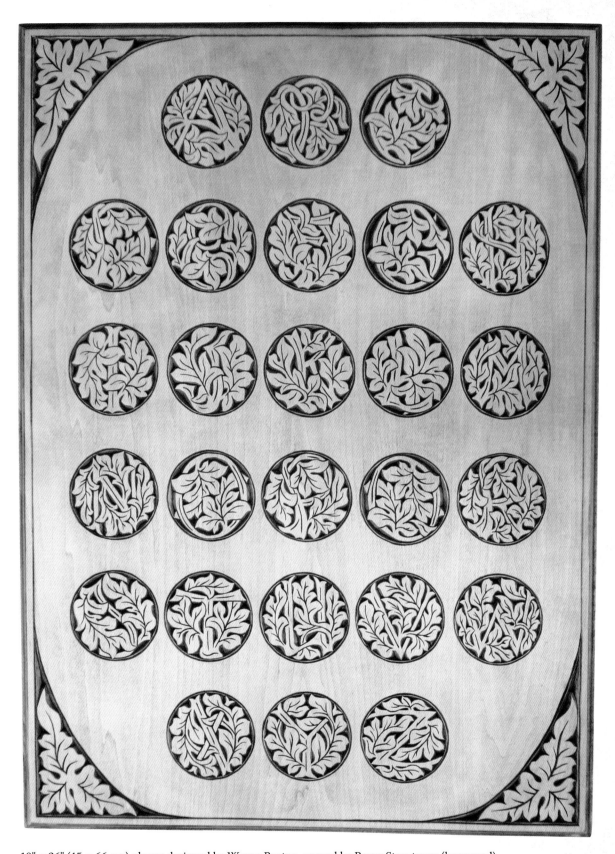

18" × 26" (45 × 66 cm) plaque designed by Wayne Barton, carved by Roger Strautman (basswood)

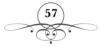

Gallery

This collection of chip carvings represents a journey through negative and positive concepts, old and new styles, and previously untried thoughts and notions of this aged art form. The variables seem endless. The challenge for the chip carver is to design and carve according to a specific area definition and configuration dictated by the parameters of the object being carved. This calls for an understanding of the elements of design pertinent to chip carving as explained in an earlier section.

Here in this section you will find familiar motifs (and some new ones) in different combinations producing different design solutions. These certainly are not the only design possibilities available to you but their study will assist in formulating your own creations in both designing and carving.

Give close observation when studying these carvings to the extensive and frequent, often subtle, use of the stab knife. Its use is found in flowers representing stamen and buds, at the end of lines and extensions thereof, and in their own small motif usually of three stabs. The varying use of the stab knife will add a delightful sparkle to many carving efforts.

Royal Charter

1. Be The Truth
2. Deliver Happiness Through Royal Service
3. Create Fun & A Little Weirdness
4. Be Kind, Generous & Thankful Everyday
5. Be Adventurous, Creative & Open Minded
6. Pursue Growth, Embrace Learning,
   & Promote Through Teaching
7. Build Open & Honest Relationships
   With Clear Communication
8. Build A Positive Team & Family Spirit
9. Be Passionate & Determined
10. Do More With Less
11. Recognize A Problem, Recommend A Solution
12. Embrace & Drive Change
13. Operate With Honesty, Empathy, Integrity,
    Gratefulness, Humility & Trust (HEIGHT)

KING ARTHUR'S TOOLS

34" × 28" (86 × 71 cm) plaque (basswood)

Roger Strautman and
Wayne Barton easily
working, right hand,
left hand

Royal Charter

1. Be The Truth
2. Deliver Happiness Through Royal Service
3. Create Fun & A Little Weirdness
4. Be Kind, Generous & Thankful Everyday
5. Be Adventurous, Creative & Open Minded
6. Pursue Growth, Embrace Learning,
   & Promote Through Teaching
7. Build Open & Honest Relationships
   With Clear Communication
8. Build A Positive Team & Family Spirit
9. Be Passionate & Determined
10. Do More With Less
11. Recognise A Problem, Recommend A Solution
12. Embrace & Drive Change
13. Operate With Honesty, Empathy, Integrity,
    Gratefulness, Humility & Trust (WEIGHT)

KING ARTHUR'S TOOLS

Roger and
Wayne finished

JOY OF CHIP CARVING

6" (15 cm) scoop plate (basswood)

12" × 4" (30 × 10 cm) practice board (basswood)

JOY OF CHIP CARVING

12" (30 cm) outside-beaded rim plate with Celtic knot border and compass rose center. (basswood)

18" × 6½" (45 × 16 cm) serving tray (basswood)

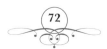

18" × 8" (45 × 20 cm)
bellows (butternut)

JOY OF CHIP CARVING

8" outside-beaded flat plate
(basswood)

8" scalloped flat plate (basswood)

18" × 5½" (45 × 14 cm) cutting board
(basswood)

24" × 6" (61 × 15 cm) plaque for garden of my wife's
aunt in Baretsvil, Switzerland. (basswood)

12" × 3" (30 × 7 cm) box front panel (basswood)

9" × 3" (23 × 7 cm) box front panel
(butternut)

8" outside-beaded flat plate with trefoil center motif. (basswood)

8" scoop plate with
quatrefoil motif. (basswood)

8" (20 cm) basket lid (basswood)

12½" × 8" (32 × 20 cm) box lid (basswood)

5" × 7½" (13 × 19 cm) box side panel (basswood)

6" (15 cm) plain edge
flat plate (basswood)

8" outside-beaded flat plate
(basswood)

8" scoop plate (basswood)

5½" × 3½" (14 × 9 cm) lidded pot (basswood)

5½" × 3½" (14 × 9 cm)
lidded pot overview (basswood)

5½" × 3½" (14 × 9 cm) lidded pot (basswood)

4" (10 cm) pot lid (basswood)

JOY OF CHIP CARVING

8" outside-beaded flat plate
(basswood)

12" scalloped beaded rim plate with positive leaf and negative ribbon border. (basswood)

16" (40 cm) rim plate American bald eagle anniversary plate (basswood)

6" (15 cm)
scoop plate (basswood)

14" (35 cm) inside scalloped
beaded rim plate (basswood)

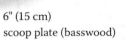

6" (15 cm)
scoop plate (basswood)

12" scalloped rim plate with floral border and Gothic rosette center. (butternut)

10" outside-beaded flat plate with floral cross. (basswood)

JOY OF CHIP CARVING

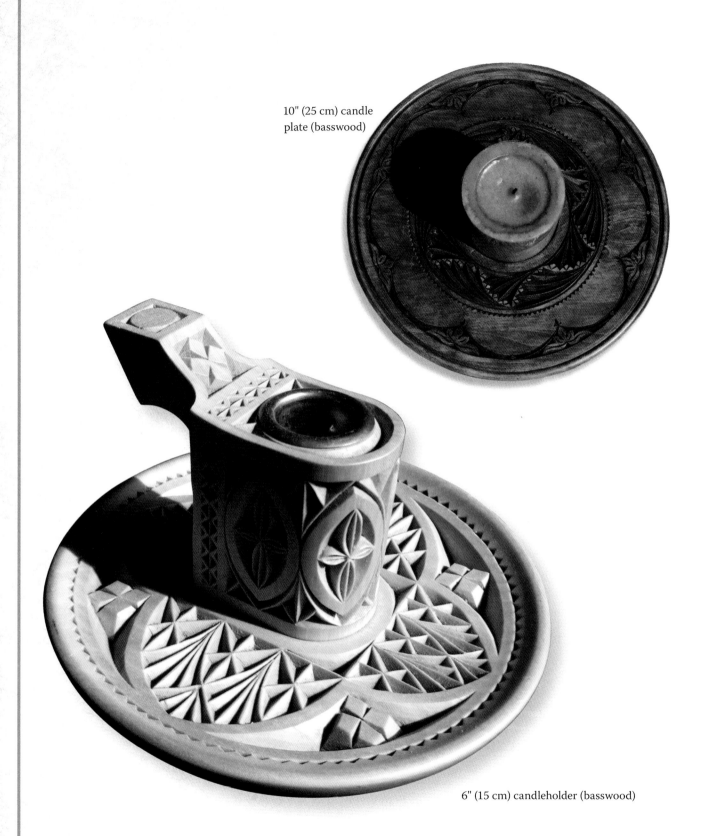

10" (25 cm) candle
plate (basswood)

6" (15 cm) candleholder (basswood)

8" (20 cm) outside
beaded flat plate
(basswood)

12" × 4" (30 × 10 cm) study of leaves (note changing the width of lines produces a third dimension appearance)
(basswood)

JOY OF CHIP CARVING

10" outside-beaded flat plate
(basswood)

10" rim plate (basswood)

JOY OF CHIP CARVING

18" × 8" (45 × 20 cm)
bellows (basswood)

12¾" × 8¼" (32 × 21 cm) box lid (Hailey is my granddaughter's name). (butternut)

10" outside-beaded scoop
plate (basswood)

10" scoop plate
(basswood)

JOY OF CHIP CARVING

12" (30 cm) scalloped oval plate
(basswood)

9" × 7" (23 × 18 cm) box lid (basswood)

8" (20 cm) outside beaded flat plate (basswood)

6" (15 cm) plain edge flat plate (basswood)

6" flat plate (basswood)

6" scoop plate
(basswood)

6" (15 cm) scoop plate (basswood)

6" (15 cm) plain edge flat plate with great blue heron. (basswood)

22" × 11½" (56 × 29 cm) plaque (butternut) . Originally carved in stone on the Church of St. Peter and St. Paul in Bern, Switzerland, the text reads, "*Machsna*," which means "Imitate this."

12½" × 8" (31 × 20 cm)
box lid (basswood)

10" (25 cm) candle
plate (basswood)

JOY OF CHIP CARVING

6" scoop plate
(basswood)

6" scoop plate
(basswood)

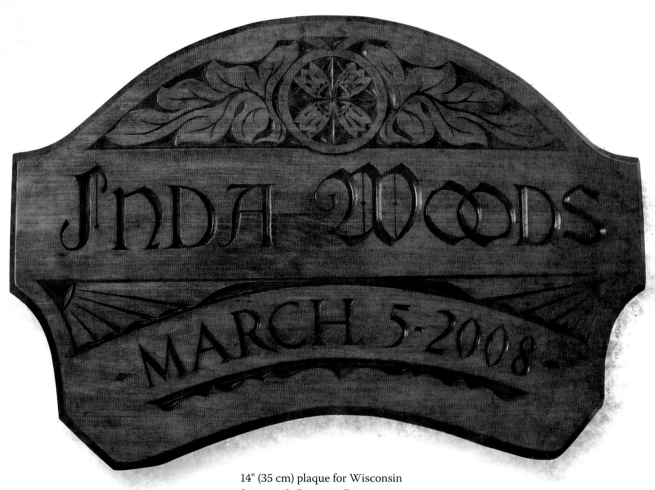

14" (35 cm) plaque for Wisconsin
farmstead. (basswood)

12½" × 8" (32 × 20 cm)
box lid (basswood)

JOY OF CHIP CARVING

10" outside-
beaded flat plate
(basswood)

JOY OF CHIP CARVING

14" (35 cm) lamp
panel (butternut)

14" (35 cm)
lamp panel
(butternut)

Lamp top plate
(butternut)

14" (35 cm)
lamp corner
view
(butternut)

JOY OF CHIP CARVING

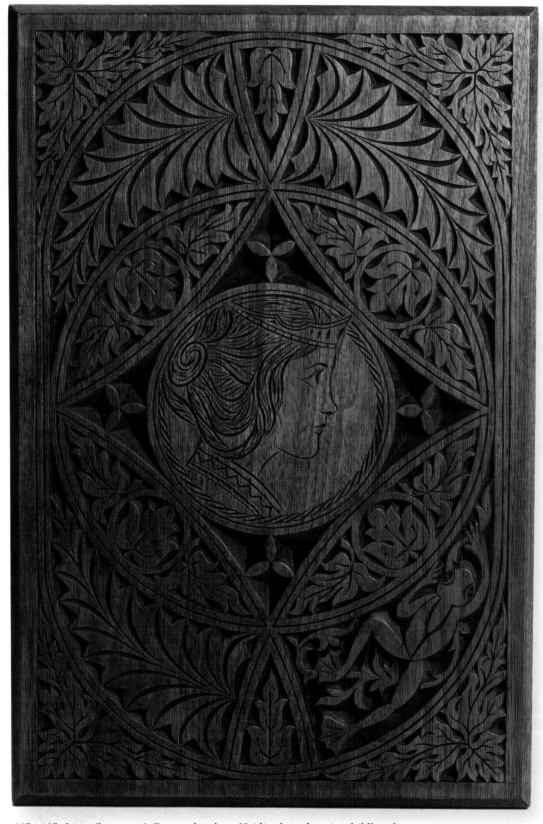

18" v 12" plaque (butternut). For my daughter, Heidi, whose favorite childhood story was "The Princess and the Frog."

9" × 7" (23 × 18 cm) box lid (butternut)

12" foxtail brush

17" × 6½" serving tray
(basswood)

9" × 7" (23 ×
18 cm) box lid
(butternut)

14" × 9" (35 × 23 cm)
cross (basswood)

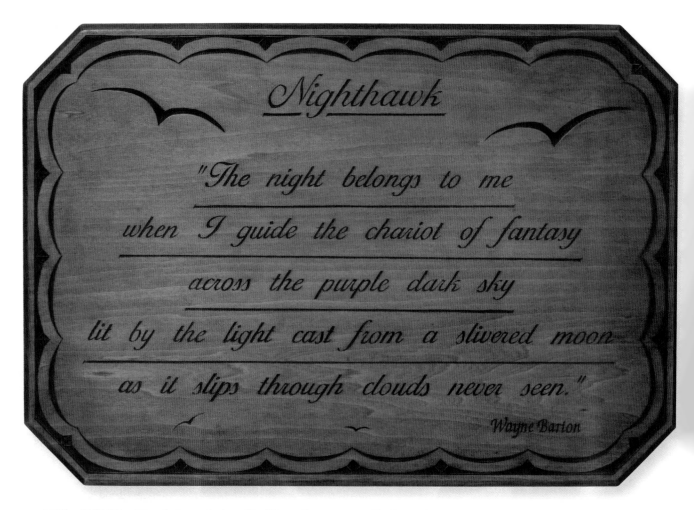

Nighthawk

"The night belongs to me
when I guide the chariot of fantasy
across the purple dark sky
lit by the light cast from a slivered moon
as it slips through clouds never seen."

Wayne Barton

16½" × 11½" (42 × 29 cm) plaque designed by Wayne Barton, carved by Roger Strautman (basswood)

24" (61 cm) memorial cross (butternut)

Octagon box overview
(butternut)

Octagon box panel
(butternut)

7" (18 cm) octagon box lid
(butternut)

Octagon box panel
(butternut)

JOY OF CHIP CARVING

14" (35 cm) ale tray with Celtic knot design on handles. (butternut)

10" × 8" (25 × 20 cm) thistle design

10" × 8" (25 × 20 cm)
thistle (basswood)

7" × 8" (18 × 20 cm) front panel
cribbage board (basswood)

14" × 8" (35 × 20 cm)
opened cribbage
board (basswood)

8" × 4" (20 × 10 cm) chip carved version of Goddard/Townsend shell design (basswood)

12" heart plate
(basswood)

8" × 3" (20 × 7 cm) box front panel (butternut)

attern for box front panel

7" × 5" (18 × 13 cm) desk organizer panel (basswood)

7" × 5" (18 × 13 cm) desk organizer
panel (basswood)

7" × 5" (18 × 13 cm) Desk organizer
panel (basswood)

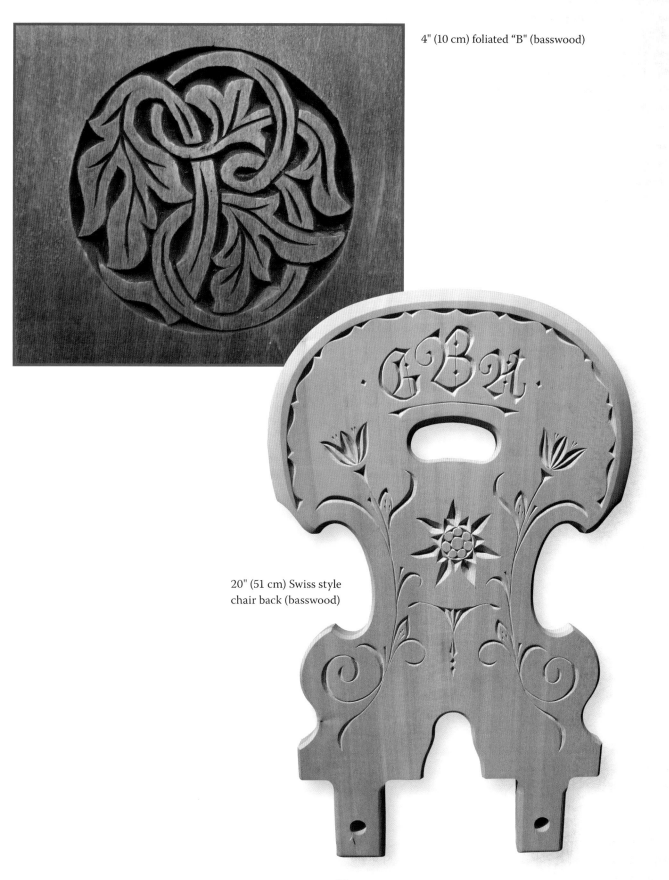

4" (10 cm) foliated "B" (basswood)

20" (51 cm) Swiss style chair back (basswood)

JOY OF CHIP CARVING

Child's rocker overview (basswood)

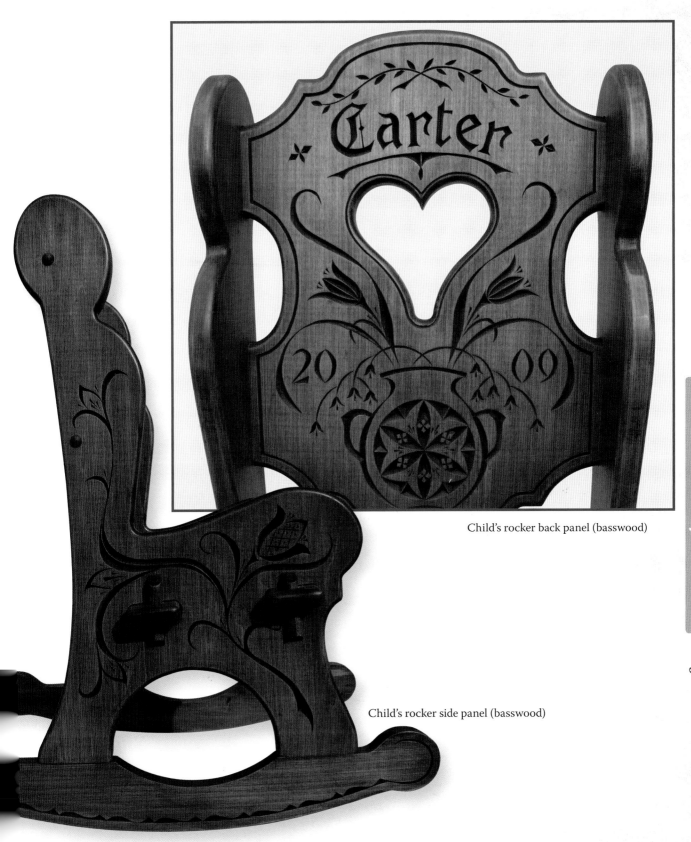

Child's rocker back panel (basswood)

Child's rocker side panel (basswood)

JOY OF CHIP CARVING

8" (20 cm) candle
plate developed by
repeating leaf pattern
four times. (basswood)

Pattern for
Candle plate

JOY OF CHIP CARVING

12" scalloped beaded rim
plate (basswood)

8" (20 cm) outside beaded flat plate
(basswood)

)" (25 cm) candle wedding plate (basswood)

16" breadboard

12" (30 cm) scalloped
beaded rim plate
(basswood)

6" (15 cm) scoop plate
(basswood)

12½" × 8" (32 × 20 cm) box lid (basswood)

9" × 7" (23 × 18 cm) box lid (butternut)

12¾" × 8" box lid
(basswood)

Pattern
for box lid

JOY OF CHIP CARVING

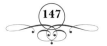

10" (25 cm) candle plate (basswood)

12" × 12" (30 × 30 cm) "Abbey" candle centerpiece (basswood)

9" (23 cm)
candleholder
(basswood)

9" (23 cm)
candleholder
(basswood)

9" (23 cm)
candleholder
(basswood)

" (23 cm)
andleholder
basswood)

JOY OF CHIP CARVING

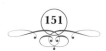

About the Author

Wayne Barton is a professional woodcarver living in Park Ridge, Illinois with his wife Marlies, their four children having left the nest. His interest in woodcarving was first kindled at the age of five by his maternal grandfather who was part of his extended family, leaving him with a lifelong love of woodcarving.

Mr. Barton is a veteran having proudly served in the United Stated Coast Guard. After military service and college, still with a desire to pursue his passion for woodcarving he took his formal woodcarving training in the woodcarving center of Brienz, Switzerland. Today, his carvings can be found in private collections in Europe, Asia, and North America. He is the only American to have chip carving in special exhibition at the Swiss national Museum in Zurich, Switzerland.

For thirty-seven years he has been a columnist for Chip Chats, magazine of the National Wood Carvers Association, and has contributed articles for Fine Woodworking, American Woodworker, Woodcarving Illustrated, and other publications. He has written seven other popular books on woodcarving and has made a number of television appearances on The American Woodshop with Scott Phillips, and The Woodwright's Shop with Roy Underhill.

Mr. Barton is the founder and Director of the Alpine School of Woodcarving, Inc., devoting much of his time to teaching throughout the United States, Canada, Norway and Switzerland. He also has designed and manufactures chip carving knives and sharpening stones recognized for their exceptional quality by enthusiasts.

Although versed in all disciplines of carving, he specializes in chip carving and has won both national and international recognition for his work and contributions to the woodcarving community in general.

For a more beginner-oriented book by Wayne Barton, look for *The Complete Guide to Chip Carving* (2007).

Wayne Barton's website is *www.chipcarving.com*.